THE MANAGER'S
POCKET GUIDE TO
GENERATION X

By Bruce Tulgan
Author of
Managing Generation X

Published by:

HRD Press
22 Amherst Road
Amherst, MA 01002
1-800-822-2801
    (U.S. and Canada)
1-413-253-3490 (Fax)
http://www.hrdpress.com

Lakewood Publications
50 South Ninth Street
Minneapolis, MN 55402
1-800-707-7769
1-612-340-4819 (FAX)
http://www.trainingsupersite.com

ISBN 0-87425-418-3

Production services by Clark Riley
Cover design by Eileen Klockars
Editorial services by Mary George

 PRINTED IN CANADA

TABLE OF CONTENTS

Case Studies: Real-Life Stories from Gen-Xers in the Workplace

Dedication

This book is dedicated to my entire family: My wife Debby Applegate; my parents Norma and Henry Tulgan; my sister Ronna and brother Jim; my brother-in-law Tom and sister-in-law Terri; my nieces Elisa, Perry, and Erin and my nephew Joey; my grandmother Gertrude; and my in-laws the Applegates—Julie, Paul, Shan, and Tanya.

Acknowledgments

I want to thank all the people—more than a thousand now—whom I've interviewed in the last four years. Thanks also to all those I've met along the way in all the companies, associations, and schools where I've been so fortunate to speak. I am blessed with so many dear friends and I feel I owe you all my deepest gratitude.

To my cohorts at RainmakerThinking, Inc., past and present, thank you for joining me in studying our generation's experience in the workplace, especially Mark Kurber, Heather Boardman, Joe Engwer, Nathaniel Antman, Jeff Katz, Homer Robinson, and Soyong Cho. No thanks would be enough to my co-managing principal here, Jeff Coombs, for Jeff is the kindest, most sincere person I have ever known, a true friend, and my alter ego in this enterprise.

Special thanks go to Soyong Cho, who helped me conceive this project and made valuable contributions to it.

Very special thanks go to Bob Carkhuff at HRD Press who recognized the value of this issue in the training and development market and chose to pursue an ongoing partnership with Rainmakerthinking, Inc. Thank you Bob—it is an honor to work with you.

To my entire family—thank you. And to my wife Debby Applegate, I couldn't face each day without you, much less write books. I am endlessly grateful to have you as a life partner.

Author's Biography

Bruce Tulgan is the founder of RainmakerThinking, Inc., a think tank which researches the working lives of Americans born after 1963. He has been a featured speaker to business leaders, managers, association members, young workers, and students all over North America and internationally. Bruce's first book, *Managing Generation X: How to Bring Out the Best in Young Talent* (Merritt, 1995), is a guide to managing rising young stars in the workplace. Bruce is also the author of *Work this Way: Inventing Your Career in the Workplace of the Future* (Hyperion, January 1998). His writing has appeared in the *New York Times* and the *Los Angeles Times*, as well as numerous other newspapers, magazines, professional journals, on-line sources, and academic publications. His work has been the subject of scores of new articles across the country and new reports on radio and television programs. While Bruce retired from the practice of law in 1994, his is still admitted to the bar in New York and Massachusetts. He has taught management on the graduate level as an Assistant Professor of Management and holds a fourth-degree black belt in Uechi Ryu Karate. Bruce lives with his wife, Debby Applegate, in New Haven, Connecticut.

Introduction

I spend most of my time interviewing Americans born between 1963 and 1977, the fifty-two million Americans known as Generation X. In those interviews, I ask Xers how they are being managed, how that is affecting their work, how they want to be managed, how they are looking at their careers, and how they are balancing their careers with the non-career aspects of their lives.

I spend most of the rest of my time sharing what I am learning about Generation X in the workplace with those who rely on Xers' time, energy, creativity, and hard work—with those who are "Managing Generation X," which is the title of my first book. I try to help managers and business leaders to understand Xers better and to bring out the best in the young people who work for them. I also try to help young workers learn how to bring out the best in themselves.

But, please don't think that this *Pocket Guide* is going to take the position that Xers have it all right and managers and business leaders have it all wrong—or that the only way to bring out the best in young workers is to bend over backwards to meet Xers' every need and expectation. My work—and our work at Rainmaker, Inc.—is not about driving a wedge deeper between the generations in the workplace, but rather about closing that gap and bringing the generations closer together to everyone's mutual benefit.

Let me explain what is at stake for most Xers in their careers: Xers are starting out their working lives in the wake of downsizing, restructuring, and reengineering. Of course, everyone is going through these profound changes in the economy—this is not unique to Generation X. The difference is that Xers are starting out their careers in the midst of all this chaos. Xers never got to play by the old rules, and Xers have no point of reference for working by the old rules. Imagine you are swimming in a big pool and the water starts draining out: Those who have made it halfway across the pool or three-quarters of the way are going to look at this dilemma much differently from those who just jumped in the pool— the water level is the same for everyone, but the experience is fundamentally different.

Xers know that they cannot rely on established institutions to be the anchors of their success and security. No one in this generation expects to base their career on a long-term affiliation with one established organization. More Xers believe in UFOs than believe they will ever receive a Social Security check. Xers know that the only success and security they can hope for is that which they build for themselves from within themselves.

But this is not a sob story. The good news is that Xers believe in their own skills and abilities. More than anyone or anything else, Xers believe in themselves. This is why most Xers see themselves as sole proprietors of their own skills and abilities. No matter where they go, no matter what they do, Xers are in business for themselves. Whether they are starting up their own companies, dropping out of the rat race, or trying to make it in a decent job in an established company, Xers are in business for themselves.

Before they turn 30, most Xers will have had at least one pretty good job and one pretty bad job. They will have dropped out of the rat race for a while, tried to start their own business, and at least considered going back to school. Often, they will be doing all those things at once. Every single year, more than 17 million Xers change full-time jobs. What are they searching for? Could it be that the whole generation is just restless?

Xers are searching for the same thing most people are searching for: success and security. The problem is that nobody knows what success and security are going to look like for our generation. So Xers are busy remapping the way to security and picking up the bits and pieces of success along the way. Xers are moving from one new experience to the next, aggressively seeking new marketable skills and knowledge, relationships with people who can help them, and creative challenges that allow them to collect tangible proof of their ability to add value in any workplace. This is the behavior I refer to as "Self Building."

Why does Self Building depend on one new experience after another? Because in a brand new experience, Xers cannot help but learn new marketable skills, meet new people who can help them, and tackle creative challenges. In a brand new experience, those Self Building dividends come at a rapid pace. Of course, over time, the pace of those dividends begins to slow down. They come further and further apart and fewer and fewer between. The dividends may be larger and more valuable when they do come, but at a certain point that becomes a matter of long–term investment.

Here is the big generational shift: It used to be that the safest path—the most risk–averse path—to achieve success was to stay in one place. In the workplace of the past, the best strategy was to make that long–term investment and wait for the larger and more valuable dividends. But in a profoundly insecure and chaotic world, long–term investments seem very risky. Xers have learned not to trust long–term investments. Rather, Xers have learned they can count on the certain flood of Self Building dividends that comes in each new experience.

It is when the pace of the dividends in one work experience begins to slow down that the job is in danger of becoming "just a job." Xers will start to look for a new focus for their Self Building energies: Maybe in a new job, or their own business, or going back to school, their social life, family, physical well being, or a hobby. The challenge for managers who want to keep Xers focused and motivated is to keep the job from ever becoming "just a job." The only way to do that is to replicate what Xers look for in new experiences—that certain flood of Self Building dividends.

It is not easy to be a worker in the post–job era. Employees can't hope anymore to work in the same old ways or follow that old fashioned career path. Today, employers need flexible workers prepared to adapt to rapidly changing circumstances and get the job done, whatever the job happens to be on any given day. To succeed in today's workforce, workers must have the ability to seize new opportunities to add value and grow personally at the same time; to quickly acclimate to new environments; to take charge of their own skill building; to stay focused on results; to monitor feedback from the world around them; and to "cash out" each day, at least figuratively, and collect the tangible rewards for their contributions of time, labor, and creativity.

The new workplace bargain Xers seek is one that recognizes that workers in today's economy are day-to-day value adders and offers tangible day-to-day rewards in exchange for daily contributions of time, labor, and creativity. Management strategies must evolve to facilitate the effectiveness of today's workers as day-to-day value adders. The rest of this *Pocket Guide* is designed to help managers do just that.

Generation X in the Workplace

1.
Generation X in the Workplace

Who is Generation X?

Generation X is the post-baby-boomer generation of Americans. Born between 1963 and 1977, they account for 33.6% of the 125 million people in the United States' workforce (as of 1996).

In what jobs and industries do they work?

Generation Xers occupy a broad spectrum of jobs, as the following list illustrates.

Occupation	Xers Percentage
Computer systems analysts & scientists	34%
Computer programmers	39.8%
Secretaries	29%
Receptionists	43%
File clerks	52.8%
Lawyers	26%
Financial service workers	36.9%
Retail & personal sales workers	50.5%
Retail cashiers	58%
Physicians	19%
Occupational therapists	49.4%
Health technicians	45.6%
Paralegals	41%
All percentages as of 1996	

Where did the term Generation X *come from?*

Generation X started as a term among advertising executives, to serve as a code word for those 52 million young Americans they considered difficult to pin down as a target market. The term achieved mainstream notoriety in 1991 with the publication of

---

AWARENESS-RAISING QUESTIONNAIRE: REALITY CHECK

Test your knowledge of Generation Xers by responding to the questions below.

1. Upon entering the workforce, what is the most important incentive Xers look for from employers?

   A. Lifelong security with one company.
   B. Opportunities to develop skills that will help them on their next job.
   C. Money.

2. Xers grew up during an information and technology revolution affecting entertainment, telecommunications, education, and everyday home life. What was the impact on most Xers?

   A. They developed short attention spans.
   B. They became disenfranchised cynics.
   C. They developed a unique comfort and facility with information and technology.

Continued

AWARENESS-RAISING QUESTIONNAIRE: REALITY CHECK (*continued*)

3. Some perceive Xers as being disloyal. What reality does this perception reflect?

   A. Job security is dead and dues-paying is an obsolete concept.
   B. Xers are immature and arrogant.
   C. Xers want to climb the corporate ladder as fast as possible.

4. Many Xers spent a great deal of time alone as children, either because both of their parents worked, because their parents did not live together, or because their parents were permissive. As a result, what is the most common personality type among Xers?

   A. Xers are nihilistic and unfocused.
   B. Xers are independent and self-reliant.
   C. Xers are neurotic and dependent.

5. Economic conditions often have a considerable impact on a generation's perspective on their economic future. What is the most common perspective among Xers regarding their economic future?

   A. They are likely to have careers based on long-term jobs in established companies.
   B. Their economic future is hopeless.
   C. They must rely on their own skills and abilities to achieve any measure of security.

Continued

AWARENESS-RAISING QUESTIONNAIRE: REALITY CHECK (*concluded*)

6. How do Gen-Xers generally view established institutions like the federal government and large companies?

   A. They are wary of institutions because they have witnessed so many institutions falter.
   B. They find institutions more trustworthy than individuals.
   C. They believe in established institutions because those institutions are powerful and efficient.

7. Xers are eager for rapid feedback and constant markings of recognition for their hard work. Why?

   A. Xers do not want to work hard for their rewards.
   B. In an uncertain world, Xers are always trying to measure the return on their investment.
   C. Xers want to get as much as they can from any situation and then exit quickly.

Reality Check Answers—1B;2C;3A;4B;5C;6A;7B

Douglas Coupland's *Generation X*, a novel about a group of cynical twenty-somethings who have dropped out of the rat race because the baby boomers have devoured all the good jobs, leaving Xers with a future of "McJobs" and "Lessness." By 1993, it was official: the successors to the baby boom were being called "X" by every major news organization and most cultural critics.

Are Generation Xers mostly "slackers" as we are told in the media?

The reason why so many people cringe when they think of Generation X is that they are thinking of a media stereotype that portrays Xers as slackers, dropping out of the rat race to live off their parents or barely surviving in low-pay, low-status, short-term jobs. Since the term *Generation X* first appeared, Xers have been described in the mainstream media as "cynical mopes," "sullen and contemptuous," "impetuous," "naive," "arrogant," "short on attention," "materialistic," and other equally unflattering variations. Surveys of the media's coverage of Generation X have concluded that the vast majority of the portrayals of Generation X have been unduly negative.

Surveys of baby boomers who are managing Xers in a variety of white-collar fields reveal that boomer-managers find Xers to be disloyal, insufficiently deferential to authority, short on attention, uncommitted to work, arrogant, unwilling to go the extra mile, and unwilling to pay their dues. These misconceptions—the slacker myth—undermine the ability of managers to maximize the potential value of Xers in the workplace.

How can we begin to understand the real Generation X?

Since childhood, Xers have been proving themselves *to themselves* by defining and solving for themselves the problems of everyday life, from making breakfast for themselves when their parents were getting ready for work, to making dinner for themselves when their

7

parents had to work late. For most Xers, coming home from school meant letting themselves in with a latchkey and keeping themselves company during the afternoon—with a microwave snack on one knee, their homework on another knee, the remote control in one hand, and the telephone in the other hand, creating a market for call waiting. As their everyday problems became more complex, they learned new problem-solving skills, their repertoires developing in sync with the information revolution. To this day, Xers' resourcefulness and comfort with information and new technologies remain critical in their efforts to cope in an uncertain world.

For Xers, opportunities for creative expression provide the psychologically important, and very practical, reassurance that they will be able to fend for themselves tomorrow just as they have during much of their childhood. Working for a living, therefore, is for Xers the most natural venue for staking out a position of safety in a dangerous world.

1. *Misconception: Xers are disloyal.*

Reality: Xers grew up in the aftermath of the baby boomers' discrediting of institutions. As Xers grew up, all of society's most important institutions were faltering—schools, cities, government, big business, religious institutions. As Xers enter the workforce, big business is going through downsizing and reengineering. Xers know that the old fashioned workplace bargain—dues-paying and loyalty for security—is obsolete.

2. *Misconception: Xers are arrogant.*

Reality: Most Xers spent a lot of time alone as children. But just because you are alone doesn't mean you face any fewer problems—it just means you face them alone. When you face problems alone, you learn to fend for yourself. Xers' intense self–confidence is not that of arrogant children, but rather that of children who learned over and over again that, if they had to, they could fend for themselves.

3. *Misconception: Xers have short attention spans.*

Reality: While all of us have been living through the information revolution, the information revolution shaped the way Xers think, learn, and communicate. Of course, Xers think, learn, and communicate differently than those who grew up prior to the information revolution. But Xers' natural inclination to multiple focus (homework, remote control, telephone) and selective elimination ("Is this going to be on the test?") makes Xers' minds well suited to the tidal wave of information and technology in which we all live.

4. *Misconception: Xers are not willing to pay dues.*

Reality: The concept of paying one's dues depends on a notion of long-term investment. Xers are used to a short-term world in which nothing is certain. They saw people break their backs in the 1980s only to land in the downsizing of the 1990s. That is why Xers are always looking for the day–to–day dividends on any investment of their only career capital—their time, labor, and creativity.

9

5. *Misconception: Xers cannot stand deferred gratification.*

Reality: Since they can remember, Xers have lived in a world where everything is changing faster than anyone can keep track. The only thing they can count on is that nothing will stay the same. So, Xers have learned to check carefully feedback from the world around them to see what is changing and what is staying the same, what is working and what is no longer working.

From Reality to Impact

The key to understanding Xers is understanding the key historical forces that have shaped this generation, what I call the four "I"s: institutions, independence, information, and immediacy. Each of these elements has a cause-and-effect pattern: the Reality and the Impact.

1. INSTITUTIONS

Reality: During their lifetime, it has become clear to Xers that they cannot rely on established institutions for long-term security.

Impact: Xers are very cautious about investing in relationships with employers, just as they are cautious about investing in relationships with any large institution. They tend toward **the entrepreneurial** and **try to invest in themselves, creating security from within**.

2. INDEPENDENCE

Reality: Xers were latchkey kids in an increasingly dangerous world, during a time when society was becoming more and more atomized. Their parents were more likely to be divorced, to both work, or to be more permissive than parents of prior generations.

Impact: Xers are used to facing problems on their own and have great confidence in their ability to fend for themselves. They tend to be **independent, goal-oriented, outside-the-box thinkers and workers** who **want to manage as much of their own time as possible**.

3. INFORMATION

Reality: Xers learned to think and communicate in the midst of a tidal wave of information. Supplied with increasingly sophisticated technology, they were able to manipulate that information with greater and greater ease.

Impact: Xers process information differently than do those of prior generations. Their facility with information and technology is likely to be the most important survival skill of the twenty-first century. Because of this facility, they tend to be **comfortable with information and technology** and **creative**.

11

4. IMMEDIACY

Reality: Xers were raised in a culture of immediacy and uncertainty.

Impact: Xers expect the world to respond quickly to their input. They monitor results so aggressively because they want feedback that will help them measure their success and adjust their approach accordingly. They tend to be **flexible—ready to adapt to new people, places, and circumstances**—as well as **eager to prove themselves** and **to see results every day.**

Generation X Is the Workforce of the Future

Looking through the lens of Generation Xers' life experiences, one starts to see a more complex picture of this generation. Of course Xers are cautious about investing in relationships with established organizations—they have no reason to expect that such relationships will pay long–term dividends. To some, this makes Xers seem disloyal, but this is also what makes Xers so amenable to the kind of short–term, day–to–day value adding that employers need from workers. It's easy to see why Xers would think, learn, and communicate differently from those of other generations. This is what makes Xers so comfortable with information and technology. Xers may be fiercely independent, but this is what makes them so entrepreneurial and such independent problem solvers. Xers are always trying to monitor the world around them for fast feedback. This is what makes them so adaptable to change.

Think about this more complex picture of Generation X: This is a familiar profile, but it is not a familiar profile of Generation X. It is a profile of the kind of worker that every management expert and every business leader has been saying organizations are going to need to compete and succeed in the changing economy. It is a profile of the kind of worker every individual is going to have to become in order to survive in the workplace of the future. Maybe the punch line is: "Be careful what you wish for." The workforce of the future has arrived, and it's Generation X.

While it is probably true that every new generation of workers clashes with the generations in power, Xers' clash coincides with the most profound changes in the economy since the industrial revolution. Xers are shaped by the very same forces shaping the workplace of the future, and Xers are uniquely well suited to lead organizations into that economy.

— Profile: Generation X Worker of the Future —

√ **Flexible—ready to adapt to new people, places, and circumstances**

√ **Comfortable with information and technology**

√ **Outside-the-box thinker and worker**

√ **Independent**

√ **Wants to manage as much of his or her own time as possible**

√ **Goal-oriented**

√ **Entrepreneurial**

√ **Creative**

√ **Eager to prove him or herself**

√ **Wants to see results every day**

√ **Tries to invest in self, create security from within**

2.
Recruiting and Selecting the Stars of Generation X

There are four key elements to recruiting and selecting the stars of Generation X: (1) Creating a profile of the ideal applicant for the position to be filled; (2) Developing a recruiting message which will be effective in attracting applicants who meet that profile; (3) Selecting the person most suitable for the job from among all the applicants; and (4) Ensuring that the applicant selected is given an accurate preview of the day-to-day experience of the job he or she is being hired to do.

(1) *Profiling the ideal applicant.* There are several factors to look for in an applicant for any job: Raw talent, learned skills and knowledge, relevant work experience, ability to learn the kinds of skills and knowledge necessary to do the job, and willingness to devote substantial time and energy to the tasks and responsibilities of the job. In order to profile the ideal candidate, use each of these categories to identify the particular traits and characteristics necessary to the particular job in question.

Profile Builder	Raw Talent	Learned Skills & Knowledge	Relevant Experience	Ability to Learn Key Skills & Knowledge	Willing to Devote Time and Energy to Tasks and Responsibilities
Specific traits and characteristics needed for this job					

(2) *Developing an effective recruiting message.* Xers are looking for several key factors in a job: Opportunities to learn marketable skills, to build relationships with people who can help them, to tackle creative challenges, to produce tangible results and collect proof of their ability to add value in any workplace, and to manage as much of their own time as possible. In order to build the right message to attract the best applicants, use these categories to inventory the opportunities held within the particular job you have to offer.

Message Builder	Learn Marketable Skills	Build Valuable Relationships	Tackle Creative Challenges	Produce Tangible Results	Manage Own Time
Specific opportunities within this job.					

(3) *Selecting the most suitable person.* Once you have attracted several ideal applicants, the challenge is to select the most suitable person for the job in question. In order to do so, you will need to use some of the traditional techniques such as reviewing resumes and cover letters, conducting interviews, and checking references.

In order to select the best Generation Xers, you will also need to put aside some obsolete assumptions. For example, it is no longer wise to dismiss an applicant merely because he or she seems to be a "job-hopper"—someone who has not held any one job for more than one or two years. This is no longer an indication of someone who is unable to get along and contribute in the workplace, but rather may indicate someone who has unique skills and is able to apply those skills on short-term projects to meet immediate and ephemeral needs. Such an employee may be very valuable in today's economy of uncertain markets and unpredictable staffing needs.

Let me suggest two important strategies which will tell you a great deal about whether or not the applicant is the kind of day-to-day value adder you need: (i) Ask for free samples of tangible results accomplished by the applicant in prior experiences (make sure you have some way to verify that the tangible results were in fact achieved by the applicant); and (ii) Ask the applicant to submit a written proposal describing exactly how he or she would apply his or her skills to meet a specific need in your organization.

(4) *Providing an accurate job preview.* One of the most common causes of voluntary turnover is when new employees find out that the job they were hired

17

to do is not exactly what they envisioned when they applied. The best remedy is to make sure that, once you have selected the person who seems to be most suitable for the job, you provide that person with an accurate preview of the actual day-to-day experience of accomplishing the tasks and responsibilities of the job. Let me suggest five approaches to providing an accurate job preview: (i) Offer the applicant you wish to select the opportunity to "tag along" with another person in your organization who is doing the same (or similar) job. By tagging along for several days, a week, or more, your applicant will get a good picture of what the job actually entails. (ii) Produce a videotape of someone in your organization performing the key tasks and responsibilities of the job and provide an opportunity to view the tape. (iii) Create a written (and illustrated) document instead of a videotape to achieve similar results at a lower cost and provide the applicant with a chance to thoroughly review the written document. (iv) Engage the applicant in a very frank discussion describing the specific details of the key tasks and responsibilities of doing the job. (v) Let the applicant engage in frank discussions with several people who are actually doing the job and instruct them to be painfully honest about the low points as well as the high points of the experience.

3.
Orientation for New Employees—
Sending the Right Message

***What is the right "welcome" message to send to
newly hired Gen-Xers?***

Let's say you have recruited the right people and are
now ready to conduct an orientation program with
them. What approach should you take? In general,
the answer is *the realistic approach.* It is no longer
credible to say "welcome to the family" as if new
employees can expect to be part of the company for
the rest of their lives. Remember that most of your
new hires know that the only kind of career security
they are ever going to achieve is the kind they create
from within themselves.

That is why Xers think of themselves as sole
proprietors, no matter where they work. Xers look at
every job as an opportunity to trade their skills,
creativity, and hard work for some measurable
increase in their self-based career security. Xers
think in terms of a new implicit workplace bargain
based on daily win-win exchanges. They wish to add
value for employers who are willing to reward them
daily with Self Building incentives (relationships,
learning opportunities, and creative challenges).

𝒳 THE WRONG MESSAGES TO SEND NEW XER EMPLOYEES

1. Welcome to the family.
2. Pay your dues and you will climb the ladder.
3. There are people with whom you are supposed to interact, and people with whom you are not supposed to interact.
4. We will define your training agenda and we will train you.
5. There is a long line of people who would love to have this job, so it would be easy to replace you.

✓ THE RIGHT MESSAGES TO SEND NEW XER EMPLOYEES

1. We hope to have a win-win relationship, regardless of the length of your stay here.
2. We want you to pursue our corporate goals in a way that helps you pursue your own goals.
3. Many of the relationships you build with individuals here are likely to outlive your tenure with this company.
4. Pursue as much knowledge and as many skills as you possibly can while you are here . . . and we will do our best to make learning resources available to you.
5. We value your hard work as an individual, as well as your creativity and innovation.

4.
Communicating with Gen-Xers in the Workplace

How do Gen-Xers deal with communication and information?

The most ironic misperception of Xers is that they have short attention spans and do not deal well with information. Xers do think, learn, and communicate differently than members of previous generations, because their minds were shaped by the information revolution. That is why Xers often seem to move from one non sequitur to another; appear to resist linear thinking; sometimes don't seem to be paying attention; focus on many things at one time; prefer audio, video, and computer media; flip through reams of printed information very quickly, assimilating and discarding information with little apparent rhyme or reason; and so on. The flip side of the communication gap is that Xers' style of thinking, learning, and communicating is more attuned to the twenty-first century than the old fashioned way. You have to think fast and loose in a chaotic world.

Instead of disparaging Xers' communication style, managers should maximize Xers' unique comfort and skill with information and info-technology by making some slight adjustments in their communication practices. And they should always remember: Xers have voracious appetites for information and learning.

THE FOUR KEYS TO EFFECTIVE COMMUNICATION WITH XERS AT WORK

1. **Maintain open lines of communication.**

   Schedule time every day or several times per week for brief detail-oriented communication sessions to review projects; provide updates on managerial issues; establish and adjust work goals and deadlines; monitor results; answer questions and resolve problems.

2. **Build a rich information environment that facilitates ongoing learning.**

   Provide multiple learning resources in diverse media; encourage Xers to set their own concrete learning objectives in the context of structured self-study programs; and allow Xers to process information and meet learning objectives at their own rapid pace.

3. **Encourage everyone in your company to be a teacher.**

   Create a learning environment by making teaching part of every person's job. Teaching should not draw core personnel away from their core tasks; rather, teaching should enhance productivity all around. When teaching Xers, share information and methods of practice without dictating unnecessary rules; try to let Xers learn by doing; inspire Xers to define problems, engage their innovative powers, and come up with creative solutions.

4. **Challenge Xers with new projects demanding fresh skills.**

   Expose Xers to diverse facets of the business by allowing lateral moves to new skill areas. Armed with new skills and motivated by the learning process, Xers will gladly assume new responsibilities and meet challenges with greater productivity and initiative.

BRAINSTORMING EXERCISE: COMMUNICATING WITH XERS

Work through the four keys to effective communication with Gen-Xers in the workplace. For each key, identify THREE ACTIONS you can take to put that communication key into practice.

1. Maintain open lines of communication. Possible actions:

(a) _____
_____.

(b) _____
_____.

(c) _____
_____.

2. Build a rich information environment that facilitates ongoing learning. Possible actions:

(a) _____
_____.

(b) _____
_____.

(c) _____
_____.

Continued

**BRAINSTORMING EXERCISE:
COMMUNICATING WITH XERS (concluded)**

3. Encourage everyone in your company to be a teacher. Possible actions:

(a) _____

_____.

(b) _____

_____.

(c) _____

_____.

4. Challenge Xers with new projects demanding fresh skills. Possible actions:

(a) _____

_____.

(b) _____

_____.

(c) _____

_____.

5.
Training Gen-Xers in the Workplace

How has growing up during the information revolution affected Xers' style of learning?

Xers are shrewd and avid information consumers. They want to choose from a continuous flow of messages from multiple information resources that they control (imagine the model of 50 cable-television channels and a remote control).

It is critical to balance the company's need to have employees achieve concrete learning outcomes and attain core competencies with Xers' style of learning and information consumption.

**BRAINSTORMING EXERCISE:
TRAINING GEN-XERS**

Work through the training needs of a particular employee or a particular set of tasks and responsibilities.

1. Clarify the core competencies required to perform the tasks and responsibilities:

_____

_____

_____

Continued

**BRAINSTORMING EXERCISE:
TRAINING GEN-XERS (continued)**

2. Define the key learning objectives necessary to attain those core competencies and set concrete deadlines for reaching each key learning objective.

KEY OBJECTIVE   DEADLINE

_____

_____

_____

3. What are the key intermediate steps that must be achieved along the way to reaching each key learning objective?

KEY OBJECTIVE   INTERMEDIATE STEPS

_____   _____

                                 _____

                                 _____

                                 _____

                                 _____

_____   _____

                                 _____

                                 _____

                                 _____

                                 _____

_____   _____

                                 _____

                                 _____

                                 _____

Continued

**BRAINSTORMING EXERCISE:
TRAINING GEN-XERS (concluded)**

4. Inventory every learning resource you can make available to help Xers achieve those key objectives (books, articles, old files, sample documents, data; research tools, databases, libraries; knowledgeable individuals; real life experiences).

_____

_____

_____

Give Xers the Remote Control

Now that you have (a) clarified the core competencies you require your employees to attain, (b) defined the key learning objectives and set concrete deadlines for reaching each objective, (c) outlined the intermediate steps along the way to each objective, and (d) identified all the learning resources you can make available—you are ready to **GIVE XERS THE REMOTE CONTROL**. Give Xers access to every learning resource you can pull together and let them process those resources in their own way and at their own pace in order to reach each objective by the deadline you have set. Help Xers make a step-by-step learning plan to reach each objective by giving them a copy of the outline you have prepared setting out the intermediate steps along the way to reaching each objective.

By providing maximum learning resources and giving Xers the remote control, you will empower

Xers and give them ownership of the training process. You will also create the conditions necessary for Xers to continue learning this way on an ongoing basis as long as they are working for you.

SELF-ASSESSMENT QUESTIONNAIRE: COMMUNICATION AND TRAINING

Assess the communication/training situation in your company by responding to the questions below.

1. In your company, what resources are available to Xers when they are faced with a problem or question?

    A. They can seek out managers at all levels.
    B. They can seek out their peers for support.
    C. They have many people and information resources available to them.

2. In your company, what is the best way to describe the information resources available?

    A. Readily accessible multimedia resources.
    B. Multimedia resources, but not readily accessible.
    C. Readily accessible resources, but not multimedia.

3. Which statement best describes the approach to training in your company?

    A. Employees are trained in knowledge and skills they need to do their job.
    B. Employees are encouraged to seek opportunities to learn and develop new skills, whether or not those skills relate directly to the employee's current responsibilities in his or her current job.

Continued

**SELF-ASSESSMENT QUESTIONNAIRE:
COMMUNICATION AND TRAINING (concluded)**

  C. Employees learn on the job, without any formal
    training programs.

4. When it comes to work assignments in your company,
 what is the typical range of Xers' work assignments?

  A. They are assigned work in only one skill area at a
    time.
  B. They are assigned work across multiple skill areas.
  C. They are assigned work in only one skill area at a
    time, but are exposed to multiple skill areas.

5. In your company, what is the typical format of training
 programs?

  A. Standardized training courses/modules with
    standardized materials.
  B. Self-study courses in which employees have
    information from multiple sources, have set
    concrete learning goals, and achieve those
    objectives at their own pace.
  C. Apprenticeship-style learning primarily by
    experience.

Review your answers and take a moment to evaluate
the current state of communication and training in
your organization.

6.
Mentoring Generation X

Generation Xers are so fiercely independent that sometimes more experienced workers assume that Xers are not interested in having mentors. The truth is that most Xers place a high value on opportunities to build lasting relationships with those in the workplace who have grown wise through experience. While information and technology have usually been Xers' most reliable problem-solving resources, teachers have usually been Xers' primary human supporters outside of family (and sometimes including family). Most Xers welcome the chance to create long-term bonds of loyalty with teaching managers and mentors, especially in a world where they cannot believe in long-term bonds of loyalty with established organizations.

Xers rarely turn to mentors for raw information they can find elsewhere. What Xers look for from mentors is the kind of learning that is not available from other sources:

- Someone they can look to as a role model;
- Someone who will teach them and share experiences with them;
- Someone who will care about them and help answer some of their deepest questions;
- Someone who will push them and demand more of them than they may demand of themselves;
- Someone who believes they are capable of achieving the impossible and is willing to help them do it;

31

- Someone who will provide them with unique opportunities to prove themselves;
- Someone who will introduce them to others;
- Someone who will value their opinions and ideas, seek their input, and learn from them.

By mentoring Xers, managers demonstrate a deep commitment and provide valuable direct support to Xers' Self Building process and also win Xers' most dedicated efforts. Plus, being a role model keeps the pressure on you to always be at your very best; teaching helps you think of new ways of looking at problems and solving them; and having a protégé forces you to practice your leadership skills—priority setting, communication, and motivation.

7.
Gen-Xers and Corporate Culture

Just as Generation Xers are close readers of cultural signs outside the workplace, Xers are close readers of the signals conveyed by corporate culture. Xers are always looking for evidence that investing in a particular employer–employee relationship is worthwhile, or not. That is how Xers decide whether a job is "just a job," or has the potential to be something more. When Xers see in the signals of a given corporate culture that a company's leadership undervalues the individual and treats its young workers like easily replaceable cogs in the machine, Xers feel rejected. Xers know they can never thrive in companies like that. In response, Xers reject the company and its management by psychologically compartmentalizing the job and diminishing its overall significance in their lives. The result is sinking morale, lower productivity, and higher turnover.

The goal of building an Xer friendly corporate culture is to let Xers know that your company should be the primary outlet for their creative energy. To break down the wall between Xers' jobs and the rest of their lives, you have to convince Xers that your company is a worthwhile focal point of their personal growth.

THE FOUR FEATURES OF CORPORATE CULTURE THAT MATTER MOST TO XERS

1. ### Authority based on credibility

   Gen-Xers appreciate managers who keep well informed about employees' work and remain engaged without imposing on the creative process.

2. ### Valuing employee input

   When Xers' ideas, opinions, and work are regularly included, Xers are more likely to go out of their way to support goals and implement decisions.

3. ### Supporting individual stars and champion teams

   Xers thrive on the shared purpose and emotional/ creative support of work teams driven by individual accomplishment.

4. ### A little care and feeding

   Xers know that companies have to be lean and mean to survive, but a little fat provides insulation, allows the body to absorb critical nutrients, and prevents the burning of efficient muscle tissue under strain. Try to be generous with low cost/high return fringes like refreshments, exercise breaks, dress down days, and "fun budgets."

BRAINSTORMING EXERCISE:
GEN-XERS AND CORPORATE CULTURE

Work through the four features of corporate culture that are most desirable to Gen-Xers.

For each feature, identify THREE ACTIONS you can take to put that feature into practice.

1. Authority based on credibility. Possible actions:

(a) _____
_____.

(b) _____
_____.

(c) _____
_____.

2. Valuing employee input. Possible actions:

(a) _____
_____.

(b) _____
_____.

(c) _____
_____.

Continued

**BRAINSTORMING EXERCISE:
GEN-XERS AND CORPORATE CULTURE (concluded)**

3. Supporting individual stars and champion teams.
Possible actions:

(a) _____

_____.

(b) _____

_____.

(c) _____

_____.

4. A little care and feeding. Possible actions:

(a) _____

_____.

(b) _____

_____.

(c) _____

_____.

8.
Managing the Creative Process of Gen-Xers

Teach Xers to Micromanage Themselves

Xers have a strong need to experience a day-to-day sense of accomplishment—to confirm for themselves each day that they are achieving tangible results. This is how Xers prove themselves *to themselves* and affirm their ability to add value. The problem is that sometimes it is very difficult for new, less experienced employees to give themselves that daily sense of achievement. Maybe you've had one of those days where you run around from dawn to dusk and then, at the end of the day, find yourself asking, "What did I do today?" If you have ever had one of those days, you know how frustrating it can be. For Xers, it can be very demoralizing and have a notable effect on productivity.

Sometimes the discrete tasks in a job are so ad hoc, it is hard to appreciate them. In other cases, projects may be so big that achievement cycles are too long term for newer employees to see the smaller stages of accomplishment along the way. When it comes to very new employees, it may just be that they don't understand the job well enough yet to see the smaller tangible results they are achieving each day.

Whatever the reason, you don't want to fall into this trap: If Xers are not experiencing a daily sense of accomplishment, their morale will sink and their productivity will drop off. When that happens, they start to seem like "problem employees." Often, managers will respond to this kind of slump by managing the "problem employee" more and more closely, constricting that employee's freedom and responsibility, and checking up more and more frequently. When a manager starts doing this, he or she is going right down the path to micromanagement.

If you micromanage Xers, you will send them out the door as fast as they can find another job. The irony is that the best way to keep Xers focused and motivated is to teach them to micromanage themselves. Help Xers carve up their jobs into bite-sized chunks—help them identify all the different categories in which their tasks and responsibilities fall. For example, if your employee is a salesperson, you might carve up the job into these categories: adding names to a prospect list, making cold calls, making second-round calls, sending follow-up materials, scheduling in-person meetings with hot leads, drafting proposed contracts, meeting in-person with hot leads, closing deals.

Once you help your Xer employees carve up their jobs into bite-sized chunks, encourage them to set daily goals for themselves in each category so they can monitor their success each day. You can encourage them to do this by reminding them now and then or by helping them create a daily action planning tool like this one:

Micromanage Yourself™ Daily Action Planner for a Salesperson

Bite-Sized Chunks	Daily Goals	Daily Results
Adding names to prospect list	add 10 names	✔
Cold calls	make 10 cold calls	✔
Second-round calls	call back 5 people from yesterday	talked with 3 people, left 2 messages
Sending follow-up materials	send follow-up materials to everyone who doesn't hang up on me (at least 10 people)	sent follow-up materials to 8 people
Schedule in-person meetings with hot leads	schedule 1 in-person meeting	scheduled meeting with Ms. Brown
Drafting proposed contracts	draft contract for hot lead, Ms. Jones	got halfway through contract
Meeting in person with hot leads	have lunch with Mr. Smith	✔
Closing deals	close deal with Mr. Smith at lunch	Mr. Smith wants to think it over

THE FOUR KEYS TO MANAGING XERS' CREATIVE PROCESS

1. **Establish clear ownership of tangible end-results.**

   Devote the upfront time necessary to make explicit distinctions between end-results that belong to Xers and those that do not. Often, achieving this clarity necessitates the early dissection of projects into more clearly delineated segments—a management tool that is, in itself, altogether useful. No matter how miniscule, the tangible end-results for which you assign 100% responsibility will be an Xer's proving ground.

2. **Establish clear parameters and concrete deadlines.**

   Once ownership for each end-result is assigned, Xers will be glad to follow directions, stay within parameters, adhere to guidelines, and meet specifications, as long as they are spelled out at the time of goal-setting. Always establish an explicit deadline for each end-result.

3. **Help Xers carve up tangible end-results into bite-sized chunks.**

   When Xers can set their own daily goals for concrete results that can be achieved in less than a day, they stay focused and motivated.

4. **Ensure there is flexibility between goal-setting and deadlines.**

   In between goal-setting and deadlines, Xers want the day-to-day decision-making power to define problems, take risks, make mistakes, invent new approaches and creative solutions, and reap benefits in terms of personal growth and innovation.

9.
Giving Gen-Xers the Fast Feedback They Need

How do we understand Xers' need for feedback?

Most organizations still rely on six-month and twelve-month reviews as their primary method of performance evaluation. These formal reviews vary a great deal in format and style, but any way you slice it, Generation Xers see very little connection between their work and formal reviews of any kind.

Here is what Xers say about formal reviews:

1. Formal reviews happen so infrequently, they almost never provide feedback that is accurate, specific, and timely.
2. Often, managers and employees use the review process to protect their own interests and, therefore, reviews are usually not as candid as they should be.
3. Reviews often reflect personality issues, rather than performance evaluations.
4. Reviews create unrealistic expectations with respect to raises and promotions.

Xers see their relationships with employers as day-to-day mutual exchanges of added value. Xers invest their time, labor, and creativity. Employers provide regular short-term dividends. But those dividends can't always be in the form of money. F*A*S*T Feedback™ is one of the short-term dividends most sought by Xers in their pursuit of Self Building career security. Instead of six- and twelve-month performance reviews, give Xers F*A*S*T Feedback™.

F*A*S*T is an acronym = Frequent, Accurate, Specific, and Timely

Frequent = Provide feedback every time Xers complete a tangible result.

Accurate = Double check yourself before you praise or critique Xers' work.

Specific = Focus your evaluation on details and provide guidelines for improvement.

Timely = Give feedback immediately while your comments still seem relevant.

BRAINSTORMING EXERCISE: FAST FEEDBACK

Do you give Xers feedback that is FAST—frequent, accurate, specific, and timely? Think about a particular Xer in your workplace and his or her most recent tangible result. Then ask yourself the questions below. Repeat the exercise, focusing on different Xers.

Recent Result	Fast Frequent	Fast Accurate	Fast Specific	Fast Timely
	When was the last feedback session?	Are you certain you are talking with the right person about the right tangible result?	Are you very clear about exactly what was done right and exactly what could be improved and how?	Are you offering the feedback within hours or days of the deadline for the tangible result?

SELF-ASSESSMENT QUESTIONNAIRE: CULTURE, CREATIVE PROCESS, AND FEEDBACK

Assess your company's culture and its practices regarding the creative process and feedback by responding to the questions below.

1. Which statement best captures your company's workplace philosophy?

   A. We celebrate the success of individuals, rewarding hard work, productivity, and creativity.
   B. The company is a team, and everyone shares credit and blame equally.
   C. We place the greatest value on loyalty and seniority.

2. Which statement best describes the management structure in your company?

   A. There are several layers of management between the lowest and the highest.
   B. There are few layers of management, and junior people deal directly with senior people.
   C. Employees are managed on the same project by several managers at different levels.

3. Which statement best describes the knowledge base of the managers in your company?

   A. Managers maintain a close awareness of the work they are managing because they have done it themselves and they remain involved enough to understand the obstacles their employees face.

Continued

SELF-ASSESSMENT QUESTIONNAIRE: CULTURE, CREATIVE PROCESS, AND FEEDBACK (continued)

   B. Often managers are managing work they have never actually done themselves.
   C. Managers usually manage work they have done themselves at one time, but often the nature of the work has changed since they did it themselves.

4. In your company, how are work teams structured?

   A. They are given a clear mission with clear parameters and have one strong leader.
   B. They are given a clear mission with clear parameters, but do not have one strong leader.
   C. They have a strong leader, but often their mission is fluid and the parameters change.

5. In your company, how are important decisions made?

   A. At the top with little input from lower-level people.
   B. At the top with input from those employees who will be affected by the decision.
   C. Input from all employees is sought and decisions are achieved by consensus.

6. In your company, how are projects generally managed?

   A. After goals and deadlines are set, managers help employees throughout the process, requiring them to check in at each stage before moving on.

Continued

44

SELF-ASSESSMENT QUESTIONNAIRE: CULTURE, CREATIVE PROCESS, AND FEEDBACK (concluded)

   B. After goals and deadlines are set with clear parameters, managers allow employees the freedom to achieve the goals within the established time frame, but remain available if employees have questions.
   C. When goals and deadlines are assigned, parameters are left unclear so that employees are free to use their creative imaginations.

7. How often do you provide some type of feedback to your Gen-X employees?

   A. Daily
   B. Weekly
   C. Monthly or longer

8. How do you provide feedback to Gen-X employees?

   A. Formal performance reviews based on prearranged criteria.
   B. Informal discussions periodically based on mutually understood but unspoken criteria.
   C. Immediately and in detail, based on the strengths and weaknesses of employees' specific work products.

Review your answers and take a moment to evaluate the current state of your organization with respect to culture, creative process, and feedback.

10.
There Is More Than Money at the Bottom Line

When I speak to business leaders and managers all over North America, the question I am asked most often is this: "Are Xers really motivated by anything other than money?" The answer is an emphatic "YES." Of course, Xers want to be fairly remunerated for the work they do. Who doesn't? What is more, if the job ever becomes "just a job," then money will be the most important incentive in a manager's repertoire. But, Xers want much more than money out of work. Work is critical to Xers' self-definition and sense of well-being because it is Xers' greatest opportunity to build a new kind of success and security from within themselves. That means that managers have it within their power to provide non-financial incentives which are profoundly important to Xers.

The non-financial incentives most sought by Xers are Self Building incentives:

- Learning new marketable skills and knowledge;
- Building long-term relationships with individuals who can help them;
- Tackling creative challenges and collecting proof of their ability to add value in any workplace.

47

If you are an empowering manager and have created the conditions for effective delegation, you can send Xers' motivation level into the stratosphere by offering these Self Building bonus incentives:

- Greater responsibility for tangible results;
- Increased creative freedom;
- More power to plan their own work schedules.

Self Building Incentives Brainstorming Exercise

You can create your own Self Building incentives and bonus incentives packages by doing a thorough inventory of all the latent Self Building opportunities already available in your organization and then positioning those opportunities as non-financial rewards.

Create Your Own Self Building Incentives Package

	Marketable Skills	Relationships	Creative Challenges
Inventory latent opportunities in your organization			

Create Your Own Self Building Bonus Incentives Package

	Greater Responsibility	Increased Creative Freedom	More Control Over Schedules
Inventory latent opportunities in your organization			

11.
A New Approach to Retention: Leaving without Really Leaving

Recruiting new employees can be time consuming and expensive. Sometimes, you have to recruit two or three or four employees just to add one new high-performing value-adder to the team—someone who is going to stick around for a while. Then you have to train them and that costs money. It can take anywhere from six to twenty-four months before new employees earn more for an organization than they cost. If you are losing employees inside the first two years, you may be getting a zero return on your recruiting and training investment. That's a problem. Granted, there are some employees you are probably happy to bid good riddance. But, what about the solid performers, and worst of all, the rising stars?

Look at the top four reasons why solid performers and rising stars leave their jobs in established organizations:

1. To devote more time to their personal and family lives.
2. To pursue a better job (greater responsibility, creative freedom, more flexible schedule, new learning opportunities, more money).
3. To go back to school for an advanced degree.
4. To start a business.

There are many ways for an organization to entice valued employees to stay. You can offer them raises, promotions, benefits, learning opportunities, and creative challenges. But, if they want to leave, let them leave . . . without really leaving.

The fact is, you can probably hold on to many of the solid performers and rising stars who leave. . . if you are willing to employ them on a more flexible basis.

Why can't they leave their positions as full-time employees, but still add value on a part-time basis, or as flextimers, telecommuters, periodic temps, or consultants? After all, you've already invested in recruiting and training them. They know the organization and the people in it. They have some valuable skills and experience.

Leverage your investment: Most will be happy for the opportunity to take on as much work as they can fit into their lives and they'll do as good a job as ever. Probably even better.

12.
Management Pitfalls:
Avoiding the Most Common Complaints

Learning from the Mistakes of Failed Management Relationships

The bad management syndromes about which Xers complain the most have a common denominator: each attacks Xers' individuality and personal power in their work and Xers' corresponding pursuit of Self Building and self-based career-security. While the management practices highlighted here would not be welcomed by any worker of any age in any workplace, they are uniquely intolerable to Xers.

These bad management syndromes fall into six categories:

1. Poor time management;
2. Micromanagement;
3. Fear-based management;
4. Management without adequate feedback;
5. Unwelcoming corporate cultures;
6. Poor communication.

Let's take a closer look at each category.

Poor Time Management

Some managers insist on maintaining control over Xers' time, but fail to plan time and resources so that Xers' work goals can be coordinated with their managers' requirements.

𝒳 TIME MANAGEMENT PITFALLS TO AVOID

1. Holding onto deadlines until the last minute, making Xers wait around all day and run around all night.

2. Holding up Xers' productivity by taking excessive turn-around time reviewing Xers' intermediate results.

3. Understaffing projects so that everyone is frantic and people must be pulled away from other assignments to fill the gaps.

4. Keeping Xers around late in order to justify inflating fees based on billable hours.

5. Demanding Xers' "face time"/staying late just because the corporate culture frowns on leaving early.

6. Engaging Xers in gofer-weekends at the hands of managers who still don't know how to operate the photocopier and the fax machine.

Micromanagement

If managers want to maximize Xers' productivity, they would be wise to encourage Xers' entrepreneurial spirit. Too many managers try to control Xers' every movement, squelching their creative impulses and denying them any responsibility for tangible end-products.

𝒳 MICROMANAGEMENT PITFALLS TO AVOID

1. Devoting insufficient time to senior-level work as a result of focusing on the most mundane tasks.

2. Second-guessing results and halting final products by insisting on round after round of changes.

3. Looking over shoulders and nit-picking details.

4. Denying Xers any responsibility for tangible end-results or even a chance to add real value to the final product.

5. Reducing the hard work of two or more people to the productivity rate of one micromanager.

Fear-Based Management

Xers interpret abusive managers in terms of what they know about other abusers, assuming that a manager's abusive behavior has more to do with his or her own psychological issues than it has to do with Xers' actual work performance.

 FEAR-BASED MANAGEMENT PITFALLS TO AVOID

1. Using employees as an outlet for venting frustrations that are unrelated to the employees' work.

2. Using a loud voice, insulting words, or intimidating body language to make any point whatsoever.

3. Evaluating Xers as individuals, instead of evaluating their end-products.

4. Sending mixed messages by allowing personal mood swings to masquerade as spontaneous performance evaluation.

5. Unpredictable outbursts, which make it impossible for Xers to prepare and condition their behavior to accommodate their managers' authority.

Management without Adequate Feedback

Because Xers know that job security is dead, they seek investment-friendly environments in which they can use their creative talents to achieve the kind of Self Building that will add to their long-term security. Xers cannot invest without short-term feedback, credit, and rewards to confirm that they are not wasting their time and energy—their limited reservoir of career capital.

𝒳 INADEQUATE FEEDBACK PITFALLS TO AVOID

1. Integrating Xers' work into end-products and failing to give Xers credit for their contributions.

2. Providing no instantaneous feedback, positive or negative.

3. Spotlighting failure without making sufficient time to celebrate success and accomplishment.

4. Withholding recognition, thanks, credit, or reward.

5. Relying on formal reviews as the primary vehicle for feedback.

Unwelcoming Corporate Cultures

When Xers see in the signals of a given corporate culture that a company's leadership undervalues the individual and treats its young workers like easily replaceable cogs in the machine, they know it is not an environment in which they can thrive. In response, Xers reject the company and its management by psychologically compartmentalizing the job and diminishing its overall significance in their lives. The result is sinking morale, lower productivity, and higher turnover.

The goal of building an Xer-friendly corporate culture is to let Xers know that your company should be the primary outlet for their creative energy. To break down the wall between Xers' jobs and the rest of their lives, you have to convince Xers that your company is a worthwhile focal point of their personal growth.

χ CORPORATE CULTURE PITFALLS TO AVOID

1. Treating individuals as interchangeable and replaceable: Xers don't want to be the paper plates of the job market.

2. Too many layers of management: Xers get caught in the middle, answering in all directions, trying to manage all those managers.

3. Teams with no clear mission and weak leaders: the worst of both worlds—autonomy sacrificed for directionless teams where Xers produce less value and receive less credit.

4. Inadequate diversity efforts: Xers cannot feel comfortable where their peers are not welcome.

Poor Communication

Xers are used to the information environment of mass culture and higher education—information environments that encourage voracious consumption. They are accustomed to leveraging information as a problem-solving resource as well as a security blanket to achieve comfort amidst instability. Xers have a hard time thriving in closed information environments, with poor lines of communication and environments that do not support learning.

𝒳   COMMUNICATION PITFALLS TO AVOID

1. Giving vague instructions while having very specific expectations.

2. Providing information on an "as needed" basis only.

3. Treating questions as unimportant interruptions.

4. Controlling training resources and dispensing training in limited doses.

5. Front-loading training in the early stages of employment without keeping up the pace of training.

13.
Champion Teams and Individual Stars

How do you build team spirit in a climate of rapid change and intense competition? That challenge seems even greater when some or all of your team members are fiercely independent Generation Xers— accustomed to solving problems in their own way and at their own pace.

Xers are so fiercely independent because most grew up spending a lot of time alone, either because their parents didn't stay married, or both parents worked, or because parents in the 1960s and 1970s just tended to be more permissive than parents in the past. This childhood of aloneness taught Xers to expect to fend for themselves. But the other side of being alone is loneliness, and most Xers also have a strong desire for connections, opportunities to build meaningful relationships around shared goals, and the chance to contribute to something of lasting value. That is why the right kind of team can be such a fantastic opportunity for Xers' growth, learning, and achievement.

What Xers Look for in a Team

1. Teams focused on solving immediate needs and producing concrete results fast.

2. Teams in which each individual is brought in because he or she has unique skills and knowledge to offer.
3. Teams in which authority is fluid and facilitative, based on who has the most skill, knowledge, and experience to deal with the specific matters at hand.
4. Teams in which each individual gets credit for his or her individual contributions.

CASE STUDIES:
Real-Life Stories from
Gen-Xers in the Workplace

14.
Case Studies:
Management Failures and Successes

The Purpose of the Case Studies

This chapter comprises 50 case studies, presented as told by Gen-Xers in the workplace. Their alternating scenarios of management failures and successes provide us with a study in contrasts—an instructive mix of experience intended to promote a better understanding of the Gen-X experience and perspective. The effectiveness of these case studies depends, in great part, on your active response to them.

For each management "bomb," apply your powers of thought, and perhaps a little ingenuity, to come up with a "solution" to the given situation. *Ask yourself . . .*

 If this situation occurred in my organization, what concrete actions might I take to resolve it?

For each management "star," consider the many ways that you too can apply the basics of this book and become a model of Gen-X management. *Ask yourself . . .*

 What concrete actions could I take to follow the example of good management portrayed in this situation?

Bombs and Stars: The Case Studies

 CASE A1 — *Four Days' Work Over the Weekend, "Have a Good Sunday"*

Associate working at a major investment bank: "You can't make anybody happy because everybody wants too much. Each senior VP on the way out the door on a Friday afternoon will give me a day's work for the weekend. The problem is there are four of them. Each of them says, 'Here, this is just one day's work, have a good Sunday.' But four of them do that, so I have four days of work over the weekend. That means I cannot give anyone what they want, and I work the entire weekend, and no one is happy. When I am overloaded like that, I can't get the satisfaction of doing a great job because I don't have time to put a bow on anything. It is difficult to produce the kind of quality I want."

 CASE A2 — *That Kind of Management Fosters Long-Term Thinking*

Strategic planner for a major retail company: "Our manager gave us the right amount of autonomy with the right amount of input and support, and he really kept up our team spirit. What made him such a good manager was that the passing on of work and sharing of burdens was very well organized. He was a good listener and he expressed himself very clearly. He was great about leading and giving us direction but still giving people ownership of their work. He showed us that he respected our time, because he was a good planner and he delegated work efficiently.

"The difference between him and bad managers I have had is that he wasn't so self-centered. . . . That kind of management style fosters long-term thinking about the job and the company. And that is self-reinforcing. We had the most incredible, productive team this company has ever seen. All of the members of our team have since been promoted in the company. Our manager was promoted to a very senior position because the company was so pleased with the results our team produced."

 ### CASE B1 — *To Be Yanked Off One Project and Just Thrown onto Another*

Engineer in an electronics company: "Management began taking people from their projects and throwing them on the tail end of another project that was in urgent need. This meant there were people who were always being thrown onto the end of something, instead of having a full team staffed on a project from beginning to end. Instead of looking for the best team for a project, they were filling in gaps.

"It is very disconcerting to be yanked off one project and just thrown onto another. For one thing, it is disorienting. For another thing, there is a period of time, maybe two months, where you are absent from the project you were working on. Plus, whenever that happened to me it sort of made me question how important the original project was that I got yanked away from.

"When a situation like this becomes routine, an imbalance seems to develop between the hardship and any kind of gains. I certainly wasn't putting in extra hours and all kinds of extra effort after it became clear that none of my needs and wants were being included. It is also hard to feel like I am on a career path when I have no control over what I am working on and have no way to direct my own goals."

 CASE B2 — *I Do Better Work If I Am Able to Do It My Way*

Circulation director for a magazine holding company: "I have a lot of respect for my manager because he is very precise about what he wants but very flexible about how he lets me get there. He might say to me, 'Here is where we are on a particular situation and we want to get to point B, the information we need is *a, b, c,* and here is why I want to look at it. Now go put that together by *z* date.' That gives me a little more freedom to approach the project. It is positive because I like to do things my way and I am producing much better work here than I would under different circumstances."

 CASE C1 — *Standing Behind Me Looking Over My Shoulder All the Time*

Temporary employee speaking of assignment as receptionist in engineering firm: "The guy who was sort of in charge of me couldn't just let me answer the phone, not that he told me exactly how he wanted the phone answered either. The first day I was there, I asked if someone could walk me through exactly how they liked the phone answered, messages taken, and just the basics. But this guy kept saying like, 'Great, you don't even know how to answer the phone.' That's not at all what I was saying, but he wouldn't even just tell me the basics. Okay, so I can just wing answering the phone. I'd done it before at other places. So this guy is just standing behind me the whole time looking over my shoulder. Practically every time the phone would ring, he would come out and just stand there watching me handle the call. Then he would duck back into his office. Come on, give me a break. I thought he was going to just tell me, 'Forget it, I'll answer the phone myself, go home,' but he didn't."

 CASE C2 — *Nobody Wanted to Let Her Down*

Retail clerk in a clothing store: "The store manager was really into supporting her people. She was great about letting us basically be in charge of the store and that worked because she had every reason to trust us. She was also really into pleasing the customer, making the customers feel special. And she instilled that in all of us. She had this almost cheerleader-like way of talking about making customers feel special, like that was the only thing that mattered. She would come up to me and say, 'Tell me something you did today to make a customer feel special.' That was constant. . . We all got into it to different degrees. I was pretty into it, especially because that was about the only thing she pushed. Like even if you made a mistake, her only question was, 'How did that impact the customer?' If it did, she would let you know that she was disappointed.

"Her other big thing was that she supported her people and we were in charge of the store. She didn't check what time we got there or what time we left. While we were there she trusted us to check inventory and make sure that merchandise was stocked and presented in a way that was attractive. We had a lot of leeway on that too. She loved it if you took extra time setting up a display to make it look good. She trusted us at the cash register. She never had to remind us to clean up at the end of the day. It felt like the store ran itself, but that's because we all stepped up and did what we were supposed to do. Nobody wanted to let her down."

 CASE D1 — *He Couldn't Even Delegate the Most Minor Things*

Support-staff person in a trade association: "My manager would have his hands all over everything. He would ask me to do something, say compose a letter. . . . I would do it and he would have corrections or additions. But that process would keep happening. . . . He would keep changing his mind, want more words changed. We would spend an hour getting out a routine letter—less than three-quarters of a page.

"Another example? Once we were putting together a binder for a trade show. It was a pretty straightforward thing, lists of names and times and some other information. Anyone with a bit of initiative and a little common sense could put together a fine product that would far exceed what was necessary. But this manager just couldn't really bring himself to delegate anything. Even with this, he ultimately did it himself and took twice as much time by involving me in it.

70

"Involving me in routine tasks like composing a letter or putting together a notebook of information is supposed to save my manager valuable time. But because he couldn't even delegate the most minor things, it became counterproductive to even have me involved, because we would just go back and forth on everything."

 CASE D2 — *He Lets Me Do the Job He Hired Me to Do*

Business development manager for a large consumer-products company: "My manager doesn't lean over my shoulder wanting to know what I am doing every minute of every day. It is very clear what I have to produce, and my manager trusts me to be professional in getting my results. He lets me do the job he hired me to do, lets me make the day-to-day decisions that I need to make, and doesn't try to baby-sit me. That gives me room to do my work the way I want to do it; it means I am approaching things my own way, and that makes me a whole lot more productive."

 CASE E1 — *She Wouldn't Believe Me Until She Tried It Herself*

Research scientist at a major university: "If I reported that an experiment didn't work, my research director wouldn't believe me until she tried it herself. So I would spend weeks trying to do an experiment and then go to her to explain that it would not work. Finally she would get mad and try it herself. Then, of course, she would say, 'You were right, it didn't

71

work.' One time, after a situation like this, I heard her saying to a bunch of people that she didn't believe a word I said until she tried the experiment herself. Why have me there at all?"

 CASE E2 — *I Can Manage My Own Time*

Consultant in a management consulting firm: "The manager sets an agenda at the first meeting and sets a series of dates by which certain goals have to be met. Other than that, we are left alone to decide on the specifics of the general problem. In between these dates, unless I want further guidance and seek it out, I don't have to see my manager at all. I know what I need to do within a certain date, and I can manage my time any way I want as long as I deliver what it is that I am responsible to deliver. That means I can approach problems in a way that brings out my best work."

 CASE F1 — *I Don't Have a Good Way of Working with Someone Who Flips Out*

Kitchen worker in a restaurant: "I didn't get too much feedback until one night when I almost lost it because I took the brunt of somebody else's mistake. The food is in the window, where the waiters pick it up. One of the waiters came up and started pulling orders off the window and shoving them back through and was getting all pissed off because the garnishes weren't just right or whatever. That's fine, I mean, I was just learning to do the job and I was glad somebody was telling me, 'Hey this isn't quite right.' Then one of the managers came in to see what was wrong, which again wasn't so bad, you know, he was just doing his job. But the cook was very upset, and he got the manager all worked up, and they both just started started yelling and swearing. I didn't overreact, but I just don't have a good way of working with someone who flips out that way. From what I heard, this cook had a reputation of flipping out big time and I just didn't need that situation. You know, I walked across the street and got another job."

 CASE F2 — *Our Training Really Mattered*

Temporary employee speaking of assignment as graphic designer in an advertising agency, which turned into a full-time job: "Even though I was there as a temp, the head of the art department was all over getting me trained up to how things are done here. I was familiar with the software and I've worked as a graphic designer before, but there are a lot of little things. Also in terms of who was who, my boss went out of his way to get me introduced around. I was there for three months or so and I definitely wanted to get on staff. Before that I had told myself I was going to freelance and temp as much as I could and that way I wouldn't be tied to any one place. . . It was the atmosphere that I found so attractive. They really give you time to learn. We were talking about training resources and my boss made an off-hand comment about the one training resource that there is almost never enough of is time. That really made an impact on me, especially because it was so clear that he meant it. You need time to really learn something and giving us time was how he showed us that our training really mattered."

 CASE G1 — *The Manager Might as Well Do the Whole Thing on His Own*

Business development associate in an entertainment company: "My manager has difficulty delegating and developing trust in the people who are working for him. In anything that really matters, he is totally involved with it and has his hands all over it. The weird thing is that he tends to focus on spelling mistakes and typos instead of being a more visionary-type guy. That makes you kind of wonder about his ultimate value to the company. If I know that my manager is going to go over every detail, rewrite every word on the page, that provides me with a huge disincentive to do a good job, to really do the best job that I can do. Why? Because I know that it really doesn't matter, because the manager is going to make the thing his own and totally rewrite it, no matter how good of a job I do. . . .

"Of course, the contrast is the manager who from the start conveys that a piece of work is going to be my responsibility—that if I don't do a great job, there isn't going to be anybody covering my back. It's me or no one. That is the best incentive to do a good job because I know the whole thing is riding on me. If a manager conveys to me that he doesn't trust my work, why the hell should I work hard for him? I'm not saying that there should be no quality check. But, let me take a stab at it. I don't mind failing and learning from that if I can have a chance to do a good job and have it matter."

CASE G2 — *I Feel Good Not Having to Punch In*

Loan specialist in a mortgage brokerage: "I like the job because there is quite a bit of freedom in terms of setting my own schedule. I appreciate that a lot because I am responsible and it is nice to be trusted enough to do my job. I feel good not having to punch in. It's a more comfortable way for me to work and it makes me a more independent entity in the company. I am expected to close a certain number of loans, and when it is busy, I am here as late as I need to be.

"What works well for me is that I can make these determinations and I can decide when to be here working at the times when I am going to be most productive. If I am super busy, it only makes sense for me to be working when I can produce at an efficient pace."

 CASE H1 — *She Yelled at Me the Way No One Should Ever Yell at Anybody*

Assistant account executive in an advertising firm: "She yelled at me the way no one should ever yell at anybody, and for really stupid things. There was something the matter with her. If something went wrong or if I did something not exactly the way she wanted, she would yell and scream, 'How could you do that? You should know that! How could you not know this?' Always for something that was really a matter of opinion or that there was no way I could know about it. I would have tears in my eyes because she would make feel like I had done these terrible, awful things, when really they were just stupid little things.

"One time we were having a conference call and my manager turns to me and says, 'Do you have that mini tape recorder? Can you bring it down?' The conference call had already started. I went really fast, grabbed the tape recorder, and I even had blank tapes. I brought it right back down to her. She asked if I had tested the tape recorder. I started to say I had tested the batteries and she completely freaked out— started yelling and screaming at me. I just thought to myself, wow, the tape recorder is fine, but she should get *her* batteries tested."

 CASE H2 — *It Is Kind of an Honor System*

Researcher in an investment information service: "The job is flexible in terms of taking time off and switching hours. You can come in when you want, just as long as you put in your work. It is kind of an honor system, and people are expected to put in their time, especially since the management is so cool about trusting us to do the work. The system gives me the flexibility to attend to certain things in my life when it works best for me, which makes me feel a lot better about being at work when I am here. I put in more time if anything, but I also choose when I am going to be here. That means I want to be at work when I am here, so I feel good about my job. I feel like they are trusting us and they are flexible in the face of people's different scheduling needs. There is a lot of mutual respect because of that."

CASE 11 — *It Was Like an Abusive Family Situation*

Employee in a cable television company: "The manager developed a pattern where he would yell at people and get them scared of him and then smooth it over, once they were scared of him. He would go nuclear, yell at us, kick us out of his office, come around and yell at us individually. Then, ten minutes later, he would come out smiling and chatting as if nothing had happened. It was a little like an abusive family situation. The people who stayed there would complain like crazy one day, and then the next day, they would say, 'He's not so bad.' Like abused children, they would find fault with themselves or with extraneous situations, so as not to have to blame the manager. On the other hand, I thought the guy was so bad that I loved watching him screw up."

 CASE 12 — *I Can Hang Out a Sign That Says "Gone Fishing"*

Account manager for a consumer products firm: "My current manager gives me my goals for what I am going to produce, and then he leaves me alone. If I produce a weekly goal in a day, a monthly goal in a week, a yearly goal in a month, I can hang out a sign that says 'Gone fishing.' It is an incentive to produce and it makes me feel like the time is mine, like I am my own boss. And, it's a whole lot better working for yourself than working for someone else."

CASE J1 — *It Makes You Feel Like a Bull in a China Shop*

Information systems manager in a consumer goods company: "This manager is extremely controlling in a really sick and twisted way. Maybe she had a 'painful childhood.' She looks for things to be wrong, like staples instead of paperclips, or the other way around. . . . Basically I am always just waiting for her to chew me out. Her style is so cruel that morale is really low. It makes you feel like a bull in a china shop. Making mistakes that would seem small to anyone else are, in our small world, pretty grave. Everyone here can tell you how they learned to do something 'right' by getting 'burned' for doing it wrong. People are really tired of it, and they are out of here like there is a revolving door. We have been working on an ongoing project for two years already, which has at least another year to go. There is a big learning curve, so it is very costly to have high turnover."

 CASE J2 — *The Decision That Goes Out of This Agency Is Basically Mine*

Staff person in a federal agency in Washington, DC: "This is one of the few jobs where my opinion really counts. My manager is responsible for the ultimate decision of the agency, but he takes his cues from me. That gives me a lot of power and has a big impact on the way I approach my work. I am creating the final product—the decision that goes out of this agency is basically mine. I take real pride in the decisions, and I work hard enough to make sure my decisions are better than the vast majority of decisions that come out of this agency."

 CASE K1 — *I Suffer from Anxiety Attacks*

Associate at a mid-sized law firm: "Nobody ever lets me know how I am doing. I would leave this job tomorrow if I could because I don't feel stable here. I am not sure how my work is, or if I am producing enough work fast enough, or anything. I am afraid of getting fired—like my job is always in danger. I suffer from anxiety attacks at work, which, of course, blocks my work incredibly. I keep feeling that maybe I am just no good at this. If somebody told me I was doing a good job, if they even said, 'Just keep working hard, you're doing OK,' I would be less likely to be thinking so much about leaving."

 CASE K2 — *I Meet with My Manager Immediately after the Results Meeting*

Junior account executive in a PR firm: "The firm has a 'results meeting' every Monday morning. We discuss the results achieved for each client the previous week. Immediately after the results meeting, I meet with my manager to plan our own agenda for the coming week. We keep identical notebooks with headings for each client on a separate page and the specific tasks that are to be accomplished by each of us for each client. We arrive at the list by reviewing the previous week's list together, seeing what each one of us has accomplished, and what needs follow-up; then we set the agenda of new tasks for each client."

CASE L1 — *Nobody Ever Gave Me a Pat on the Back*

Delivery truck driver for a package delivery service:
"We are the ones who are out there making the deliveries happen on time. I'll get a call from tracking when I am on the road. . . those are the people you call when your package isn't delivered and they can see where it is because every package has a tracking number. One time I guess it was a pretty big account and this office manager is telling tracking and customer service that they are never going to use us again if we don't find this package. Plus, the package is insured and supposedly for a lot. Anyway, so I am getting this message, which is, 'Find this package.' Not like I could just stop what I was doing. . . I had a lot of other packages to deliver. So I change my route and go back to the distribution center instead of having lunch and we found the package. Great. I thought that was great that I did that and it worked out. Come to find out that this customer is so psyched she sends a letter to the head of customer service about the people in customer service and tracking who found her package and what a great job they did and how they should be rewarded. I don't blame the customer for doing that. She didn't know I was the one who found the package. What I'm pissed off about is that I had to hear about this through the back door because nobody ever even told me, nobody ever sent me a copy of the letter, and nobody ever gave me a pat on the back or a letter in my file. That really burns my ass. Why should I kill myself again? You can't find your package? Huh. That sucks for you. Whatever."

CASE L2 — *Some Chance to Have Responsibility and a Bit of Freedom*

Telemarketer in a phone bank: "What I really respect about my boss is that she makes it very clear what we are supposed to do, what the goal is. But then it's up to me how to get the job done. My job can be pretty boring and tedious and she knows that and she goes out of her way to give us some chance to have responsibility for our own work and a bit of freedom. Nobody is glaring at me if I go get a soda or go to the bathroom. If I get on my headset and work straight through and knock out my calls and get the results we need from those calls, that's all she really cares about. I think it's really important because I have worked in other telemarketing companies and they were run like a sweat shop. . . My boss here just makes it very clear what needs to get done, how she wants certain calls made, and we sit with a trainer and go through the script for fifteen or twenty minutes before we get on the phone. After that, it's up to me."

 CASE M1 — *It Was the Manager Who Got All the Credit*

Analyst at a market research company: "They take all the credit if the work goes right and none of the responsibility if it goes wrong. These managers would get mentioned at a company meeting—their work was recognized in a big way. That was demoralizing for the people below who were really doing all the work. We couldn't believe that senior management didn't know what was going on, who was really doing the work. That was a big motivation killer."

81

CASE M2 — *He Spent a Lot of Time Making Sure I Understood Things*

Staff person in planning department of a car company: "My manager worked very closely with me, like personal tutoring on the job. He spent time making sure that I understood things. The more I learned and the more my ability grew, the more he let me take responsibility. Every time I had a question, . . . he would take the time to explain, not answer it superficially. I was able to learn a lot by working very closely and observing. It was a good feeling. I felt like part of the team and like anything I did was a contribution. It made me want to take more and more responsibility and work hard for this company. Everybody was on board."

 CASE N1 — *The Reasons Were Never Really Explained to the Employees*

Electrical design engineer: "The real turning point was when I started feeling like I worked for the company instead of being part of the company. Management did a complete reorganization of everyone's work life without ever consulting us at all, without getting input, without explaining what was happening or why. We were not included in any way at all. It did a lot of harm to morale, and everyone's productivity dropped quite a bit. For myself, I had been putting in a lot of effort, a lot of extra time and effort. My interest in doing a great job kind of dissipated because there was such a loss of control. It made me feel like the work wasn't really my problem anymore."

CASE N2 — *I Admire Him Because He Can Explain a Problem*

Associate in a large law firm: "There is one partner I admire because he can explain a problem in simple and understandable terms. He is very articulate, speaks slowly and clearly, and seems to comprehend what an associate at my level might have been exposed to at this point in his or her career.

"First of all, he tells me clearly what he wants. He will listen to any questions I have about an assignment. He is generally approachable for further questions. He is also willing to admit that he may not fully understand something, which shows me that he is still human. He will also ask me in a case like that if maybe I can help him understand."

CASE O1 — *It Was Like a Metaphor for the Whole Company*

Bond trader: "You had to sign off on supplies, they charged for coffee, you paid your own phone bill, they were very cost-cutting on everything and cheap. People were always complaining about money, that they were underpaid, that they were getting screwed. We had to pay for our own Christmas party. Collecting the $56 for the Christmas party was a real hassle. Everybody moaned and groaned and complained about the money. It was like a metaphor for the whole company. The edict of the company is that everybody is replaceable—they pay nothing for loyalty, they think that it is not a legitimate cost. They attracted mediocrity, because they underpaid people and didn't treat them well. That meant they were always hiring people who were down on their luck, usually people who were fired somewhere else for good reason."

 CASE O2 — *The Things She Says to Me Really Stick*

Research assistant in a public interest organization:
"My new manager is someone I think of as a mentor and someone who can teach me a lot. She is very demanding, but she is very willing to let me express my views and she pushes me to ask questions. If she is telling me something and I am nodding, she will stop and ask me, 'Are you sure you understand what I just said?' She is able to size up when I am struggling, when she needs to check in with me and help me understand. She always takes the time to spell things out, not in a condescending way, but in a way that is intended to make sure I genuinely understand. The things she says to me really stick. She has my respect and I gladly work hard for her."

 CASE P1 — *Just Tell Me, If I Do Something Wrong, How You Want Me To Do It*

Retail clerk: "Oh, I get plenty of feedback when I do something wrong. If a customer isn't happy, they'll just chew you right out and complain to the manager, and then the manager will just chew you right out too. We have an employee of the month plaque, although we all joke that they just take turns and make someone the employee of the month. Like, everyone gets their turn, but nobody can figure out why it's them one month instead of another month. . .

It would make a big difference if they used mistakes to really help you learn how they want things done. Plus there are plenty of times I've thought I was doing something just fine and did it that way for quite a while before somebody noticed, and then got chewed out for that, too. Just being more level headed about the whole thing would make a big difference. Just tell me, if I am doing something wrong, how you want me to do it. Go ahead and tell me if I'm doing it right too. That wouldn't be a bad thing now and then."

 CASE P2 — *If You Want Input in the Schedule, You Show Up to the Meeting*

Counter clerk in a fast-food restaurant: "The first manager I worked for was really bad even when it came to people switching hours. It was stupid. A bunch of us quit. Where I work now, my manager is great about the schedule. He owns the store and he really cares if we are happy. We have a little meeting every other Monday afternoon and, if you want to have any input in the schedule, you show up to the meeting. If you don't show up, you get the hours nobody else wants. It takes at least an hour, but we pretty much make the schedule. He just starts filling up shifts by having us raise our hands. Then he gives us ten minutes to trade shifts on certain days if we want or give each other days if someone wants to work a little more or a little less one week. Then we go around one more time and the schedule is done. If we really need to, we can trade in the middle of the week, but he definitely encourages us to get it all worked out in advance. You can really tell the difference because at my last job people were always complaining and would blow off work and just quit by not showing up. People don't really do that where I work now."

 CASE Q1 — *It Became a Question of Who Was Going to Win Out*

Paralegal: "Two different lawyers were fighting over me. Each of them would take me aside and tell me that I work for him and give me a whole bunch of work. I didn't know which one to approach or how to approach them, and I was working too many hours and too many days. I was very annoyed, not at all impressed with their lack of maturity. I thought it was a very macho mentality. It went beyond how much work there was to do and became a question of who was going to win out. I was the casualty with the way it was going. I was going to quit if the problem couldn't be resolved. Of course, eventually, because neither one of them would give in, the paralegal supervisor had to hire another paralegal to keep me from quitting."

 CASE Q2 — *The Next Time, I Would Be the One to Solve That Problem*

Information systems consultant: "There was one manager who was the best manager I have ever had anywhere. He was smart, he really knew what he was talking about, he cared and was very compassionate about the people that worked for him.

"One night I was at work at about 10 p.m., and I had been there beating my head against the wall for at least a couple of hours, working on a bear of a problem. It was during game two of the NBA finals, and I remember it well because I had to miss that game because I was working so hard. He knew I was a big basketball fan. This manager was great. He pulled up a chair and we talked a little bit about the basketball game we were missing. Then he said, 'Let's see if we can get past this problem,' and we worked on it together for about an hour, until we finally got it. He dug right into it with me, and we got it worked out and he showed me how to deal with that kind of problem.

"That experience told me a lot about this manager, and it tells you a lot about him. He was a real teacher. He knew that the next time that problem came up, I would be the guy to solve it."

 CASE R1 — *Don't You Dare Leave This Company*

Information systems consultant: "The first thing out of this manager's mouth was, 'Don't you dare leave this company in the first two years because I will lose money on you.' He told us that the company loses money on new employees and we had to stay around for more than two years, so that he could start making money on us. It turned me off to him a great deal. There were two other people with me, who talked about it with me after. Let's just say that the first opportunity that came, when the headhunters started to call . . . let's just say that I had no loyalty to him."

CASE R2 — *Input from Everyone on Everything*

Analyst in a small investment bank: "My boss always asks for input from everyone on everything. For example, we are making an office move right now. And he is so concerned about all of our commutes and how it is going to affect us. Another example: when we hired an office manager, he asked each of us for input, and afterward he asked each of us how we thought she was working out. He always wants to know what we think. Of course, that makes me feel more like I am an important part of the team."

 CASE S1 — *Nobody Takes the Review Seriously*

Retail department manager in a department store: "We have annual reviews, but basically the only unknown is how much my raise is going to be. The review itself is just a rehash, everybody covering their ass. It's just something they have to do. Nobody takes it seriously really except that everybody wants to know how much their raise is going to be."

 CASE S2 — *He Gave Me the Credit and That Really Breeds Loyalty*

Administrative assistant at an insurance company: "This one time I got a call from my boss's manager saying that a client was very bent out of shape and I had better track down my boss right away or he was going to be in deep trouble. I knew he was gone, not just for a little while, but it was Friday after lunch and I knew he had sort of slipped out for the weekend. I called him at home and we worked it out over the phone and I called the client myself, sent off the paperwork, called the benefits person who needed to follow up, and then I called my boss back and was like, 'mission accomplished.' So he called his manager to let him know that everything was okay, but he totally gave me the credit and he really didn't have to do that. But his manager even called me to say thanks and to tell me he really appreciated that I was the one to put out that fire. That really breeds loyalty."

 CASE T1 — *Welcome to the Neighborhood*

Fraud control manager for a major telecommunications company: "I dealt with a lot of hostility because I was a new person in the company and because I am black. It was just one big bowl of problems. I feel that upper management supported the attitude of the lower managers in treating me like an outsider. On one of my performance reviews, the manager actually wrote that I did not make an effort to bond with the other people at my level. It would be like if I were new in a neighborhood that wanted to keep me out and I was supposed to go around and knock on each door and say, 'Hi, I am new in the neighborhood. Welcome to the neighborhood. If there is ever anything I need, should I just feel free to call you?' How am I supposed to work in a situation like that?"

CASE T2 — *No One Feels They Get Left Out*

Admissions director in a nonprofit educational organization: "The executive director is always trying to make sure that other people are included in making decisions. Even if it is a decision that he is going to make, he includes the people that should be there. Like with a budget: everyone knows full well that he is going to decide what the budget will be and that he has his own financial considerations which might end up making the decision. But, he will still include the people who are involved with the decision. No one feels they get left out."

 CASE U1 — *Zero Women Were Promoted*

Sales associate in a retail electronics store: "I was recently up for promotion. My sales figures were higher than anyone else's and I had received very positive reviews. But I wasn't promoted. Seventeen men were promoted and zero women. I never thought I would encounter that. I mean it's the '90s. That makes me feel very discouraged and upset. I just wanted to say, 'Screw you—I'm going to leave.' But I didn't want to have sour grapes. I am very nervous about bringing up this issue because I don't want them to think I am falling back on being a woman. I want to be promoted because I am competent and capable, but I also want to be on the same playing field with the men in this company."

⭐ CASE U2 — *I Could Focus My Energy on Something Else for a Little While*

Marketing manager at a publishing company: "The company has a health center with a full gym and a whole schedule of activities like aerobics, weight training, meditation, tai chi. We were allowed an hour out of each workday to go exercise. . . . Not only was it a good break, but it made the job very upbeat. . . . I could focus my energy on something else for a little while and meet other people in the company. Being in an aerobics class, or whatever, with other people from the company, I got to see what other things were going on in other parts of the company. Not to mention, when you have seen the VP struggling to lift weights, all of a sudden he is a little less intimidating than he used to be, and that makes it easier to work for him. . . .

"The company did not believe in sick days, at least they didn't call them sick days. I had vacation time and personal time, but no sick time. They don't believe in sick people, just healthy people with personal needs."

CASE V1 — *He Has a Problem with Women*

Lawyer in a city law department: "After I was there for a while, four or five of the women lawyers came into my office, independent of each other, and told me how unhappy they were about the division chief. The general idea was that he clicks better with the guys and so they move up. He doesn't click as well with the women, so they are held back and don't get the kind of advanced work they should be getting and which they need to be getting to prove themselves. That was discouraging to me because it meant that morale was obviously really low among the women . . . . When I got there I thought, wow, this is going to be a team, this is the public sector. And yet, I now think that I was a little bit idealistic about the whole thing. That is discouraging."

 CASE V2 — *Every Team Gets a Fun Budget*

Associate in an investment bank: "At this firm, 25% of a manager's bonus was tied to case-team happiness, which was measured internally by an outside firm. There is also a big emphasis on fun. Every month every team gets a fun budget, which the project team gets to decide together how to use. Usually the junior people decide what to do with the fun budget, plan something, and then do it. This company is a much more profitable company and people are much happier and more productive than those at other investment banks where I have worked."

 CASE W1 — *She Would Always Tell Me, "You Don't Need to Know"*

Assistant account executive at an advertising agency: "She would say, 'You don't need to know what's going on.' Here is where the problem would come in: a lot of times something else would come up for my manager and she would just say, 'Cover for me,' and all of this in a frantic environment, while she is running around. So, I would try to cover her obligation and . . . have no answers for anyone because she would not have included me at all, just assured me that I couldn't be useful in a situation like that.

"Also, there would be times when some action was needed but my manager's boss couldn't find my manager—then she would come to me and expect me to know about the situation and be able to help. But all I could say was, 'Well, I wasn't really involved with that.' I hate having to say that because it made me seem useless. They must have wondered, 'What is she doing here all day?' And there I am, working like crazy, but then I look stupid because my manager won't clue me in.

"After a while, whenever I went in to put something on my manager's chair, I would try to quickly read all the other stuff on her chair so I could learn what was going on. So much of what I learned was from reading all the stuff on her chair."

☆ **CASE W2 — *We Develop an Incredible Bond as a Team***

Audit staff person in a global industrial giant: "It is sort of like AA: we are all experiencing the same thing and we all lean on each other. Everyone in this job has wanted to quit many times because there are long days, difficult challenges. But as a team, we help each other through those difficult times and help each other stay in this program. We develop an incredible bond and become a real support network for each other, which is good, because we are also a source of stress for each other.

"I rely on all of these people to leverage their experience, to give advice and help, because these are people of all nationalities and all backgrounds, and tapping into their knowledge helps me do better work. Also, I can always find someone that I can lean on, vent my frustrations to, and share whatever personal problem I might be having, which helps a lot."

 CASE X1 — *I Have Tons of Questions I Feel I Cannot Ask*

Associate at a large law firm: "A lot of my colleagues say he gives very little direction. I would never want him as my lawyer. He delegates work to people but doesn't fulfill his responsibility to supervise. Imagine being a client and having him delegate the work to someone really junior who doesn't really know what he is doing and has no guidance. That means the work is not being done competently. There were times when I had tons of questions and I felt that I couldn't ask them. If I were able to ask key questions at the right times, it would cut down my time tremendously and make my work 10 times more efficient, and if they really have a time crunch, it just seems to make more sense to do that."

CASE X2 — *He Is Very Specific, So I Know Which Things I Am Doing Well*

Associate in a large law firm: "This guy makes an effort to say thank you, and it is kind of interesting to me that it actually makes a difference. It makes a huge difference to me, especially because he is very specific when he says thank you, so you really know that he means it, and also it helps that he is so specific because I know which things I am doing well. It just feels like I have his respect and appreciation."

 CASE Y1 — *I Don't Have Time for That Right Now*

Staff person in a nonprofit foundation: "My manager always has some other place to be: 'I just don't have time for that right now.' Or, 'You're right to mention that, but that's a can of worms. Good, OK, here are the things we need to talk about right now, *a, b, c, d.*' Then, with a minute left, he will say, 'Is there anything else?' If I mention something he doesn't want to talk about, he just says there isn't enough time. 'Good seeing you, don't have time for that right now.' This is the 'too-busy tactic.'"

 CASE Y2 — *Getting Feedback the Next Day, We Knew When We Were on Target*

Research assistant in a public interest organization: "We would turn out a product and then we would get feedback the next day, often based on the reaction to the product or the news on an issue. . . . We would even hear, through our manager, when the president

95

of the organization was particularly happy with something. That also made it a lot easier to take the negative feedback when things didn't work out as well. At least, we knew when we were still on target because we were getting it right most of the time."

Subject Index

To receive more information about

- Bruce Tulgan's other books, *Managing Generation X* (Merritt, 1995) and *Work This Way* (Hyperion, 1998)
- Scheduling Bruce Tulgan for a seminar or keynote speech
- Bruce's company, RainmakerThinking, Inc., what *USA Today* calls, "that funky think tank Rainmakerthinking"
- Rainmakerthinking Inc.'s other training and development services and products

Please contact:

RainmakerThinking, Inc.
53 Lawrence Street
Suite One
New Haven, CT 06511

phone: (203) 772-2002
fax: (203) 772-0886
email: mail@rainmakerthinking.com
web: http://www.rainmakerthinking.com